A QUEEN DEFERRED

A POETIC JOURNEY
VOLUME I

PAULA SOW

METROPOLITAN COLLEGE OF NY
LIBRARY, 12TH FLOOR
431 CANAL STREET
NEW YORK, NY 10013

A Queen Deferred

A Poetic Journey, Volume 1

Paula Sow

A Queen Deferred, A Poetic Journey, Volume 1

Copyright © 2014 Paula Sow, All rights reserved.

Cover Design- Colin Lawton

ISBN: 10- 978-1503201668

ISBN 13: 150320166x

© 2014 Paula Sow. All rights Reserved.

METROPOLITAN COLLEGE OF NY
LIBRARY, 12TH FLOOR
431 CANAL STREET
NEW YORK, NY 10013

DEDICATED

To my Baby Girl, LaMasia Vashti Ali Johnson.   You left here too soon, but you went forward to ensure that your mom had a true guardian angel watching over her......

I love you, and you are forever in my heart.

My Vision for the world is one that is Spiritually Connected and inclusive, wherein all live in harmony, love, joy and abundance.

FOREWORD

When diving into, A Queen Deferred, DO so without reservation.   It is a totally interesting journey that you will embark upon with me.

Contents

Introduction —————————————————— 9

Big Heads ——————————————————— 10

sex, America's Favorite Pastime ————————— 11

A Breathe —————————————————— 13

and life goes ————————————————— 16

soul touched ————————————————— 17

who can define ———————————————— 19

when the relationship comes to an end. ————— 20

Never, no, one ———————————————— 22

#360Women ————————————————— 25

a trail of broken hearts ———————————— 28

budding flower ———————————————— 31

Stolen innocence ——————————————— 34

a special gift ————————————————— 38

how to enjoy Sex————————————————————40

short change——————————————————————43

acceptance through assimilation———————————45

Happily Jaded After————————————————————48

Tenderness——————————————————————49

Like Shade——————————————————————53

Finding my way home————————————————55

My Sister, Wife————————————————————57

Vampires——————————————————————60

In 2 Deep——————————————————————63

into me beauty I see————————————————66

when they take your voice away!—————————67

Do so completely——————————————————69

that's an ugly bruise————————————————72

you have a right to anger—————————————75

Go with a Piece of Me! ———————————————78

the third person———————————————————80

.....the more things stay the same———————————81

The power of the Pussy————————————————83

so you like Black any other time——————————86

a Queen Deferred————————————————————87

Acknowledgments————————————————————88

Introduction

I am Humbled and grateful that you have chosen to take this journey with me.   It is my opinion that I am a tower of strength, however I wasn't always.   As we are living our lives out at center stage, it has been said that, " life is no dress rehearsal".   So whatever the issue or experience is, it is happening in real time.
These experiences have created most of the works herein.
Some poems are my stories directly or they are my empathetic experiences lived vicariously through others.
These sentiments are expressed In modern day form and social jargon, while adding a tad of Old English.
It has been my literary influences in the like of Rene DeCarte and Sunday School sessions, that force my poetic voice to arrive this way at times.   It is my hope that all are encouraged, enlightened and invigorated by these works.

Cogito, ergo Sum——— I think, therefore I am
———Rene DeCarte

big heads

Inspired by JP

Above reproach,
Beyond scrutiny,
Silver spoons,
Under full moons,

Glory to have a big head,

Legislations,
Regulations,
Amendments,
Agreements,
Contracts and promissory,

Aloof on life,
More often simply grandeurs

No concern for the general wellbeing of others,

Because some people have big heads,

Who never stand in judgment,
For their Crimes,
Strut away,
Bold and contrary,
Pay a meager penance,

Let no reigns hold,
For big heads,
Do soon unfold.

---

sex, America's favorite pastime

6/25/14

10/29/14

Freak bugs,
Sex then sex,
None Impervious to its vibration,
They plummet to a relief,
Or better yet to an instant release,
Unbeknownst to their souls,
Sex leaves a footprint,
Every one, each time,
Without regard,
Sex has filled you,
Distracted in lieu,
....of a renewed you,

Enter the holy grail,
A sacred place,
But not so that it's a race,
Wade in mildly,

With caution begin,

Or hold on,

'Til a breakthrough comes from within,

Unto U,

Forego indiscriminate Sex,

America's favorite pastime...

A breathe

Dedicated-- to Larielle, and every mom, everywhere that will go the length, through the fire, to the edge and through deep water for their children....

A breathe is not a sigh of relief,

A breathe is a space in time,
Out of tragedy,
Out of adversity,
From ash,
Arises from a Petri-dish,
A breathe,

A mom finds tenacity,
She finds vibrancy,
Of every waking moment,
A mom finds opportunity,

In a breathe,

A longing heart of what pains like a life time,
A courageous spirit,
Fights Goliath,
She carries sword and shield into every battle field,

Out of a breathe,
A victory!!
Another,
then another,

Out of breathe,
Not one prisoner,
Never a closed door,
Out of a breathe,
A mom will burrow her way through steel,
Cat walk a ledge,
Cut through a tree trunk with a butter knife,
Out of a breathe,

A stolen smile,
Sweet piece of chocolate,
Yet none consoles in a breathe,

Do so much,
Leaps and bounds,
Lap after lap,
In a breathe,
A mom has a mission,

Be better,
Be more,
Get more,

All for the love of our darling children,

Decisions to preserve and protect their innocence,

To comfort them,

To bring smiles to their faces,

Decisions made in a breathe,

A moment,

'twas a space in time,

'twas a breathe just enough to tear down walls,

With the strength of 10 men,

A breathe,

From a mom,

Is all she needs,

A breathe for a mighty warrior, Queen,

A mom....

and life goes on

Dedicated to a mountain named --- Francisco --after advanced workshop momentum

In an effort to heal,
Healing takes time.
It does requires tremendous
Dedication,
Yet,
And life goes on,
Thrown far, far back,
The lack of resources,
A lack of support,
A far off mountain top,
It does not stop this journey,
And life goes on,
No one around you gives a hand,
Most distract the objectives of this course,
Others mock these efforts,
Often times minimizing it and assigning your overall actions as
insignificant,
Though the sun does rise in the morning,
And here to for, hence,
Ergo,

and life goes on..

soul touched

Before you came to my soul,
There was none with such eloquence,
None with the trembling voice of charge,
Yet fraught with love and compassion,
You brought with you, and renewed a place of pouring out,
Springing to the brim,

For the love of a soul touched,

I thought I were awakened, Alive,
So enchanted with vigor also loaded with potential,
For that is the essence of

A soul touched,

Though inside one
Can not see,
But with variety and clarity,
Doth your vibe create,
Into the paradigm,
Of a prism shifted,
From sealed,

To revealed,

This is the essence of,
A soul Touched,
Moved
And Inspired...

Basic Momentum Workshop.... Melvin Miller

who can define

7:17:14. Done 10/29/14

A variety of moves,
Some saunter,
Some sashay,
Others drag,
And there are those with swag,

If however u choose,
As u carry on about ur way,
Decide on your own,
However u delight it's ok,

Up or down,
Curly or straight,
Blown or wavvy,
Braids and buns,
It's all for fun,
Frenchie twists,
Either way,
Speak with ur hair,
Make a statement,
Say it loud...
Mine, my hair and proud!!!

Dedicated--- to every woman who has had hair insecurity

when the relationship comes to an end.

A trail of broken hearts

I stand before you, vulnerable. There is no protection for me. No beautiful recitation of magical words to invoke safety over me. No ancestor assigned to my watch. Though my infant child went on to paradise, my angel, my overseer, though she alone would be no match for the forces of this world.

Here I am subdued, thoroughly enchanted by love. Captivated by the vibration that emanates from within you. For one, it should not have come at a time when there was great desire. The need was intense, the need for warmth, caring and touch.

A helpless romantic, then Why is it? That they leave behind a trail of broken hearts,

For no, I was not ignorant, for I have seen that a time before. For I know of its treasures and am well aware of the satisfaction that arrives from it.
Without threat of hell fire, or fear of losing my seat in the hereafter and beyond, did not cause me to abstain. It was I, and I alone that stood at the ready for a renewal that was necessary. A purge came in a dream. Many years ago, my journey began.

While I couldn't imagine someone else at the current, I don't dream in someone else's path. It is you who's path p I dream in. My mind's eye can see no other.

Yearning.
As they depart and leave behind a trail of broken hearts,

Past recall, demonstrates that after a sharp pain comes, when sadness falls, and this tortured soul wrangles the night, all have gone on. They retreat to their lives that were far more important than I. They walk off and discard a loving journey once traveled by two who found solace in the comforting arms of that other.

So then how? How does the day come when paths part and no one looks back?

Discarded
Nonetheless, they leave behind a trail of broken hearts

They never remember the one that held such a big peace of their heart. Goes away without regard.

For I once wrote, Vampires come to suck you, but not your blood. For they have met their fill and departs without regard. They, with a piece of you. Some portion of your essence was gone away, never to return, never to be reciprocated.

So what then? What will the journey ahead hold? It is that none knows though it wheels tremendous anxiety & enthusiasm, but for today I will sulk and coddle myself until relief comes.

For they yet still and despite all, left a slight residue of themselves,

And will not tend to u in your fragmented state, though still they leave behind a trail of broken hearts!

Never, no, one

(Father's Day 2014)

There was never a love
No protection
Not one hug or kiss

Never, no, one

Never a smile of approval
No encouraging words through the years
Not one birthday cake

Never, no, one

Never a secret to share
No ice cream dates
Not one bed time story

Never, no, one

Never a simple joke that makes u smile when the boy hurts ur feelings
No interrogator to screen the boy callers
Not one chaperoned movie date

Never, no, one

Never the loudest voice cheering from the audience
No applause for a job well done

No one sat through that graduation speech

Never, no, one

Never who gives this woman
Not one stroll down the aisle
No proud smiles for a queen, his princess bride

Never, no, one

Never for ever gone
With a damsel left in distress
Not a single advocate to fight the battle
No one to console buckets of tears through the years

Never, no, one

For a father I never had
No just an empty void
Not one lover could fill

Never, no, one

And the truth has set ME free!!
For he was never there
No applause
Not one contrived contribution...
And for love for him,

Never, no, not one day

For My Sperm Donor
The last Crackhead standing!!
I hate U, and wouldn't flinch if u were hit by a bus!!!
JUST DON'T GET ANY ON ME!

————————————————————————————(She lives LMAO~!)

#360Women

This love song is for you!!

For all my Big, bold and beautiful!!
For my Educated, Strong and Assertive,
For my Healers and medics,
For my Fashionistas and Trend setters,

For my #360Women

For my Runway Divas that keep it right and tight on date night!!
For my Cats that drive him up when he is down,
For my super freaks delivering the only Tantric Sensual third eye opening meditative Dance,
For my heart she maintains and keeps the romance,

For my #360Women

For every single one that sits in a classroom, after a hard day at their Plantation, expanding their knowledge,
Reaching for their power, for their slice of Pie in the sky!!
For all those with Ass hole bosses that ignore the very FACT THAT they THEMSELVES are the makers OF INSTITUTIONALIZED PREJUDICE AND RACISM, the gate keepers of Sexism, the oppressors of Realism!!

For my #360women,

For my open school night advocates,
For my counselors and mediators,
For my coaches,
For my cheerleaders,
For my bake sale bakers,
For my school fundraiser,
For my rebels,
For my activist,
For every pumped fist,

For my #360Women

For my junk rump,
For my bald Bitch,
For my short chic,
For knocked kneed big foot Ish,
For my flat chested or double G breasted,
For my slim wasted,

For super-sized graces,
For my minimum wage earners,
For my lane changers,
For my weave wearers,
Big lipped bearers,
For my Mother Earth natural conscious queens,
For my brown paper bag passers, butter pecan tan,

But not light enough to stand, stand first, but a favorable first runner up,
Black girls never get chosen first,
Phat girls stand last in line,
For my black as the ace of spade, beautifully made, home grown,
envy of all...

I am you!
This love song celebrates all of you!!
For my #360Women

a trail of broken hearts

A society that is inherently exploitative,

It's not a far cry to believe that on all fronts an exploit arrives,

If even only slightly,

And how would love be any different?

How would the sensation of the manifestation of ,

Be any different,

Exploitatively,

Leaving behind,

A trail of broken hearts,

Dust we remind ourselves,

Life lives in people.

The connection between

Family,

Friend,

Foe,

Life, yes, It lives in people,

Look after one another,

Care for,

Empathize with,

Show compassion for,

Exploitative?

No,

Stop Leaving behind,

A trail of broken hearts,

For if not a mom,

Then who?

Who will love u,

Who will dedicate a time for

Your filling,

For your fueling,

For your rearing,

It is not only superficial,

It is deeply engraved,

The people they will lay to whip,

On to one another,

Exploitative,

Stop!

Leaving behind,

A trail of broken hearts,

Inside,

OJT,

On the job training,

Life is,

For this culture seeks to exploit the ignorance of others,

To subject them to second class citizenship,

Stealing their breathe,

Away goes their dreams,

Away goes their love aspirations,

Away goes their hopes and visions,

Thank yourself,

For it is you...

Who are guilty of leaving behind a trail of broken heart!!!!

Inspired by FGM...my heart grieves for these women and girls. Moved for so long and yet it sits on my heart and mind.

budding flower

To my vagina,
I love u,
   Inside of that tender place,
One lip,
Another covers over,
Inside,
A budding flower,

   The sweetest,
Most prettiest wrinkles,
All with great character,
   A gift,
From God,
   This symbol of good,

   To my vagina,
I love u,
   A budding flower,
Inside a tiny capsule,
Within the place
Where energy travels,
Surges and pulsates,

Triggers sensations,

To my vagina,
  I love u,

  Woman,
I am,
  For my vagina dust not
  Make me, me,

  It dust not control me,
For I,
And I alone,
  Make ready for usage,
Or not,

To my vagina,
  I love u,
  No one can not endear me,
  For the love of my vagina,
  It is my private place,
From in it, it emanates
A relaxing cloud,
  It makes calm at night,
Lends a relief inside of unfulfillment,

  To my vagina,

I love u,

Men come that they are ignorant,
This instance baffles their minds,
For I am the master of my clitoris,
  With it I choose not a path that is whorish !!
A treasure of great possibility,
  Why cage her,
  Why clip her wings,
  For if she dust freely give of her budding flower,
Usually it is for love,
   To my vagina,
 I love u!

Stolen Innocence

Fresh little girl
They always say,
You nasty,
Don't touch that,
Big people blamed me,
What did I do?
I didn't have a clue,

I cry out,
It is me, who has stolen innocence,

Most of them shun me,
Often times they never want talk about it,
The one person, a mom, that shoulda been an advocate,
Mischievously smiled,
She said, where is your proof?
Funny thing to say to a small child,

Now, I need a hug,
It is me, who has stolen innocence,

The family matriarch,

Had advice once,
She said,
"just put that outta yo mind",
Well I thought,
Now that's an interesting approach,
Since he's there every day,
No one came to defend that little voice,
These people act as if I made this choice,

Baffled and Confused,
It is me, who had stolen innocence,

They ravaged that little body since it was a seedling,
And has done it however they wanted,
They did to it whatever their perverse minds pleased,
Be it a mother's boyfriend, a mother's husband, a father's youngest brother, older boy cousins, that jolly neighbor, school teachers, or other trusted officials,
Grown ass men manipulating and pretending to love,
Always, and never asking me,
No one asked me,
That's not fair,
It is me, who has stolen innocence

What happens after that,
The bosom of care,
The bosom of love, I searched high and low,
Arms outstretched,
But not always good,
my minds says,
let's go,
So I will build me my own family,
She can do it,
So can I,
Blocking everyone else out,
That was his way,
She's not too swift to know,
That is how domestic abusers take your power away,
You see,
She wants love,
It was her, who had stolen innocence,

Well, that didn't work,
The universe took my precious baby,
It took my husband too,
It shattered once again,
My little family,
All because,

In the first place,

no one protected,

Nor did they coddled,

Nor did they defended,

That little girl child,

Not even this society,

It always labels you,

Second class,

Utility,

Tool,

Hoe,

Bimbo,

Tramp,

In a world like this,

How does broken little girls grow to build strong self-concepts,

How do they find value in themselves,

How do they become emotionally healthy,

What turmoil is beset before these girls turned women,

Who cares because,

From the very beginning,

She's been crying out,

It is me, who had stolen innocence

a special gift
Dedicated to Isaiah(dadu)

My young Prince!
A Ball of fright I was to look upon your sweet face.

Round, comely, full of tenderness,
Into this world u emerged.

My special gift!

In trusted with a great and mighty work,
To rear and to love and to prop up,
A wonderful King to be,
This duty I owe to u,
My young prince,
For u have my heart,

My special gift!

I celebrate you, my heart beats with unknowing and anxiety,
It finds solace in my duty I shall embark upon,
Your days, I will fill with many kisses,
And many hugs,
Your life is owed to this journey,

Along your way,
U will find circumstances of faltering,
Shrink not For I am your guide,

On this rough terrain you are equipped with vitality,

With enormous strength and endurance.

When those ones come,

And they will,

Be assured that your ancestral lineage will deliver your course,

As for now, my young prince,

You are my special gift,

I am ever thankful for your coming.

For you haven chosen me,

I, as your mom,

I am because we are,

One!!

My special gift!

how to enjoy Sex

A sweet tantalizing experience,
2 stand in the place of a singular existence,
For intense, is a breath of passion,
Rolling and rocking,

A sultry Mix of spiritual bliss,
Hold tightly,
Cling forth and pull into You,
a wet salivary kiss of pure intensity,
Plunges in mouth to mouth,

This is truly how u enjoy sex,

An immortal flame burns with the fiery of a roaring river,
Moisture delivers just the right amount of pheromones,
These adjoin the senses to make a continuous,
Pious connection betwixt the realm of spirituality and carnality,

For this is how u n joy sex,

Uhm, soft a caress,
Dig in even deeper,
Hands appear to be as a rapid follow-up,
Strong grips couple salivary kisses;
Passion, on him as he gazes on her,

Eyes submit,
Moans say yes,
Please, into a trance of absolute,

Into an ever radiant luster of milk and honey,
Pour out of this tantalizing unity,
An outburst of purity,
Devoid of any pollutants,
Just a sheer,
Love coalesce merging into one force,
One rhythmic vibe,
One pelvic stride,
Together inside the universe,
Spell bound and encapsulated,
Thrusts deep into the abyss
Of submission to,
Given each other his whole,
Her hole,
Selves,
Conceding one into the other,
Uninhibited,
Fulfilling every erotic desire as the mood moves,
For she giveth him and he giveth her,

For this is the only way to enjoy sex,
That will be the conduit into

A profound intimacy,

So reach,
Dig deep,
Into your lover,
Present ur sexual vibration,
To usher in a unified spiritual experience,
Passed beyond the act of sex,
And forth into absolute,
Unconditionally, strong waves that through love,
breech the sound barrier,

This humbly offer to your love,

It is in fact, the only way to,
Truly, enjoy sex!!

short change

Raise your hand if they pass you short change,

I often wonder,
Is this it!
As I gaze, eyes squinted,
And my countenance baffled,
What is this?
Is it that I should accept this
Short change...

Look at my face,
For if u could see the place of my heart, you will not pass me,
Short change,

After I have given my all,
Only presented my very best,
As without reserve or the side that's skimpiest,
The largest piece,
But unto the honesty of my heart,
Take this crap,
I don't do short change,

Remember when you called upon my name,
A valiant stage doth I come,

That I may appease your request!
For then I, at one occasion, I do apprehensively, bashfully,
Attempt that I would,
A meager asking, If I may propose...
So then, and y must I,
In return for my efforts,
Receive,

Short change,

For I don't accept short change,
It would be that I do think highly of myself,
That it is I,
Who hath a misconception of mine own importance,
Strangely enough,
Many before me,
Live in utter bliss,
With their lives, filled with short change,

Although, for it is no task that I ask, that I myself am not inclined to return,

So it is my proclamation,
That I shan't accept short change, as I do not pass off short change, as full tender!!!

acceptance through assimilation

My beauty is set on high,

Placed at the pinnacle,

Simply added to the list of obstacles,

You are set above the masses,

It is your duty to free all the other classes,

It is your commitment to our ancestors,

Proud of your lineage,

To stand tall,

Forging forward,

Never wavering at all,

For a time the only escape was within,

Deeper and deeper,

Into the belly of the whale,

Inside of the fiery furnace,

Once the only choice was assimilation,

For u,

For me,

It's not likely we will ever see,

A single soul offer recompense,

Not for sure an admission

Of empathy,

Not the slightest degree of humanity,

They have fooled the lot of them,

They so ardently blame the victim,

With this a conditioned response,

Manage your mind,

You will need to react in kind,

Self-preservation is the first cardinal rule of life,

For your exhausting work,

For your toils in the field,

It is my decree,

An exact answer for this historic atrocity,

Answer because my beauty is set on high,

Shift the chalice,

Pour out a mighty hand,

A grand blow,

Awaken, friend, family and foe,

Alert the world,

In my skin, I illuminate,

I radiate the essence of one commonality,

One universal measure,

one blood,

One heart,

One mind,

Living in that beautiful skin,

Rejecting acceptance through assimilation.

Happily Jaded After

Happily Jaded After------ after what? After we have received our 2 piece and a biscuit and there we have moved to the sunny side of the street.

The first Black this

The first woman that

This is a piecemeal and a jaded appeal for compromise.

With these accolades come a manner of prestige, with that prestige comes compliance.

The first this or first that hasn't stopped our young people from being gunned down by local government officials, all across this country.

If in fact all things being equal, it would not be a need for these distinctions. Black this, female that, first this...have we entered a place of Happily Jaded After------After what? After we have received our 2 piece and a biscuit and there we have moved to the sunny side of the street.

We compete, competes still for the most simplest of human needs.

Yet for some, a celebration ensues, preceded that was long suffering blood dripping sweat, deluded by the praise of anticipation ...

Yet segregation, dehumanization, effeminization, followed by meditations within an inadequate education... The structuring that do in fact prohibits your blackation !!!

Happily Jaded After------After what? After we have received our 2 piece and a biscuit and there we have moved to the sunny side of the street.

If in fact a latent Black president turned the tables of racism, I would be a monkey's ass!

For in truth a black president serves the enculturation of assimilation, a far cry from true identification...

We are Happily Jaded After------After what? After we have received our 2 piece and a biscuit and there we have moved to the sunny side of the street.

~~~~~~

Tenderness

Don't coddle that tenderness,

Don't flaunt it,

Diminish,

Wither away and die,

They say,

Don't behave that way,

Tighten your chin,

Lest the undesirable will befall you,

Onsite it is an odd phenomena,

Unfamiliarity,

Peculiarity,

Is the prognosis,

Crazy,

Is the proclamation,

Raw form,

Rough uncut,

Untainted,

Preserved at its most pristine form,

The remnants of innocence remain,

In the face of those woes,

What would u do,

Or U,

Or U,

A rapid display of love and kindness,

Bright smiles to mark its residence,

Warm embraces as signature of its levity,

This my heart,

This my wholeness,

This my truth,

This is my love,

Trials, tribulations, character assassinations,

All manner of violations this tenderness did weathered,

Derived out of the face of adversity,

A beckon of love for all of humanity,

A many detest this display,

Envy, their eyes convey,

You had a choice,

You have a choice,

But instead you give credence to the voices,

The Nay Sayers,

The Haters,

The Undelivered,

Those Drowning in despair and sorrow,

These are your counsel,

Why did u let go of ur purity,

And Replaced it with this life's insanity,

As This little child's heart and mind is tender,

Tenderness,

When u have the privilege to be graced by it,

Adore it,

Coddle it,

Fortify it,

Experience it,

Cultivate and Unleash your own tenderness!

For all in the world to see,

It is the only saving grace,

Lest we all perish under the bow of this treacherous existence,

Give your tenderness,

Wholly and fully,

Without reservation,

For if when I arrive I shan't appear Alien!

For love and kindness will beget a brighter destiny for us all!!

Like Shade

Like shade a retreat,

A haven for relief,

Glided is what he did,

Walking is too carnal for this love,

A statue that is larger than life,

An elevated glow with furious intensity,

A glimmer of charge and Law,

Radiates from his pours,

Only for a spell to grasp such an array of grandeur,

Like shade a retreat,

A haven for relief,

Humbly I honor,

My essence we are of one origin,

He is the continuum of,

The extension of,

The completion of,

His shade, he is shade,

A retreat,

A haven of relief,

Escaped slimly the trenches of his plight,

What has become of the black man's plight in America?

He has delivered such a breathe,

A stress like non-other,

Duress but still his heart roars like thunder,

My shade, he is shade,

Like shade a retreat,

A haven for relief,

Found in your arms,

The legacy of preceding travelers,

Those bestowed upon you a great and vital work,

Let it stand,

Restore the impetus to atop these vertices,

Forgo the pitfalls of this important call,

For your duty is with grave significance,

They shan't levy your efforts in support of a contrived illusion,

Make haste with diligence into your Crown,

For I honor and support you,

Leveraging your works with strategic maneuvers,

You are adored and celebrated,

Truth from the center,

Like shade a retreat,

A haven for relief!

Finding my way home

A lingering yearning persist,

Restful sleep no more,

Just a constant open sore,

A lasting longing,

To be there,

To feel that,

To fall into the bosom of that loving embrace,

A grueling journey,

Finding my way home,

Had they not made such an adulterated lie of my history,

It would have never become an obsessive journey,

Unlocking those buried truths,

Those clues that will awaken the essence,

A grueling journey,

Finding my way home,

To that land,

To where kings and queens walk,

Where my ancestors reigned glorious,

Where the cradle of all humanity arose,

A grueling journey,

Finding my way home

Once said, u can't miss something u never had,

For It is coded within the depths of my unconscious mind,

My people, I want them,

Do they want me,

Are they aware that I am excavating,

Toiling daily,

To beat a path to the lap of my fathers,

Where men stand tall,

Where children play,

Where women have strong leaders and are protected every day,

Where elders happily sing,

blessing births and marriage rings,

A people with one voice prays,

A commitment to community,

A grueling journey,

Finding my way home!

A rich tapestry of enormous proportions,

Centuries of that vibration,

It runs through this people,

My people, I am,

A constant frequency,

Home,

I live a grueling journey,

Finding my way home!!!

My Sister, Wife

This heart is for u,

Your tears are not in vain,

For I feel your pain,

The fundamental learning of our youth was inadequate,

The trip across an imperfect life,

Enduring mountains of strife,

In the shadows,

Owing to the world and never to ourselves,

Our small portion does span outside of our individual homes,

Therefore I see your grind,

No worries I always send you good vibes,

My sister,

Wife,

This heart is for you,

My sister,

My hand,

Please take it,

You're not alone,

Stress not, no more late night tears,

No more painful moans,

Chin up,

My sister,

wife,

You have akin through our bonds and mutual life,

We share laughs and girl talks,

Your held up,

utilize me as support, however u need me,

Trust me emotionally,

My sister,

wife,

This heart is for you,

This mold is an age old tradition,

Your obedience strengthens family relations,

Empowers and fortifies platforms for the next generation,

Forsake not your duty,

I am forever in your corner

My sister,

Wife-

This heart is for you.

Dedicated to Rivkah and Nzingah

Vampires

The vampires they come to suck u but not ur blood

It's when they sit around u n soak u up,

When they hang on your every word,

Studying ur language,

Cataloging your anguish,

Their true intentions are never fully known,

The vampires they come to suck u, but not your blood,

They come to Pierce your Aura,

Not to suck your blood,

Blood is reminiscent to your life force,

The source that delivers nutrients to every cell in your body,

Oxygen,

They come for the very life force that defines you,

Your soul,

They will drain u dry of your,

life force,

They will kill, they will steal, they will destroy, the vampires they come to suck you, but not your blood,

Face 2 face as friend,

Rendering advise with good intent,

Though erasing your choice,

Playing men as mice,

While lost in the sauce you file for divorce,

Robs you of your lover,

Challenging you into the depths of your self-esteem,

The vampires they come to suck u, but not your blood,

It will sing to enchant u,

Whisper to you in your sleep,

Coddle the weak,

                  Maneuvers ever so gently through your children,

                      Placing in their heads allowable sins,

                      Fills you with frivolousness, foolishness,

                        It owns space in your mind,

                          In your walk,

                          In your talk,

                          Exploits your ignorance,

                          Blinds your good sense,

                      Makes you tolerant to injustice,

                Resigns you to silence for senseless violence,

          The media vampires they come to suck u but not ur blood

                            Paranoid they say,

Conspirator they list you,

Blacklisted, redlined,

Ostracized in

Shit knee deep,

The vampires they come to suck you, but not your blood.

In 2 Deep

With every rolling tide,

And every single stride,

My view from the valley,

Encourages me to have a selfie rally,

Debunked, Discarded,

Abandoned,

Diminished and invalidated,

My love not worthy,

Left in the wilderness to wither and wallow In forever gone,

My heart said we are in 2 deep,

My selfie rally

Agenda to compete,

To complete the work,

To stay abreast and journey the intense landscape,

To unleash on the world all manner of magnificence,

For they discarded, abandoned,

Diminished and invalidated, a well full,

Filled to the brim with deliberate talents,

Bubbling over with exceeding goodness,

My heart it said, we are in 2 deep,

My view from the valley,

As deep as the oceans bed,

Wide enough that the Grand Canyon Blushes of envy,

Tumultuous weeds,

It By mere chance, I still breathe,

With none, not a single drop of romance,

Sick, nasty, guttural, repugnant,

Was that view from the valley,

Until a humble voice utters,

We are in 2 deep,

For with every single tear,

A spring of anxiety,

A spring of inadequacy,

A spring of righteous indignation,

Pours from the depths of a sad place,

A mad place,

Retrospect Into my creation, my origin,

Thought provoking doubt lodged within,

To by which cup must I continue to sip,

For which cross must I repetitiously carry up a steep hill,

Beatin' with the cruel stick of time,

Abruptly, with great vigor,

Must I fight the battle for strength they say,

To what and how dust this thorn Pierce,

For of the innocent, did I arise,

should I make this penance,

Is it my doing that hath given such a blistering travel,

Into this tangled web of no,

None, gone,

Though still it persist, my voice, bellowing out, we are in 2 deep,

I hear again, my voice says,

We are in 2 deep 2 QUIT!

into me beauty I see

What is this rendering?

A blatant disregard?

Am I here,

Do I stand overlooked?

Passed by,

The one who is gone on to Fly,

was she not woman?

Is she not beautiful just the same?

Not the same,

The only standard way of simple minds is that which is a mindless acceptance of Standard as the norm,

The only form.....is that of conformity,

I can remedy this because,

Into me beauty I see!

When they take your voice away!

Stifled, not silent...!

The mind wonders,

The heart reaches,

For an outlet,

A way to reveal,

A way to purge it out,

When they take your voice away,

Muffled under pinched lips,

Grin and bare it,

A tight lip,

A split tongue,

Thoughts resolve to a world wind of Insurrection,

For without release,

Air is restricted,

Love, life and happiness,

All placed in detention,

It happens when they take your voice away,

Stomache churns,

Sweat crawls down your back,

The beat is strong,

Constant,

Anxious,

A thumping in the temple,

Always when, they take your voice away,

Atop the pinnacle,

On your soap box,

Utter vehemently,

To give free those tortured tails,

To alarm of the great unveil,

Bring in the light,

For only a fortnight,

Doth you pardon,

For fear and fright,

Lay into the beast,

A great and mighty arm,

Cuz, For ne'er again, shall they take your voice away!!

Do so completely

When you adore me,

Do so completely,

The list of that multi-faceted me,

That eclectic trinity,

Queen, Mother, Woman,

Know by the light that glimmers within,

When u court me,

Do so completely,

Don't hold back,

Steadfast to explore,

Get lost in the waves of

Of forever more,

more, more,

She is the one that has depths unseen,

Undiscovered,

This lady, a true testament to the folly that is this earth's walk,

Insodoing,

Arises more refined,

Though multiple,

Still offering the love that is undeniable,

If you are loved by her,

U surely find yourself ever full,

Heart soothed by her gentle touch,

Skin tingles under the massage of her caress,

Sweat pours from the delicious dance of tantric sex,

For when you love me,

Do so completely,

A woman fashioned only by the heavens,

Venus herself stroked her soul,

Embodies to be the pillar for all humanity,

For the desires of many,

Stands a list,

Though when that blessing comes uniquely packaged,

A face turned away,

So when u stand before me,

Do so completely,

A modest presentation,

Though the resolution is sharp,

A graceful glide,

Though moves gently,

however deliberately,

consistently as to be accompanied by djembe drums,

the sweet soft pluck of a harp, hips steadily roll,

Tall with a high head,

Exudes royalty with each step,

Shoulders back,

Chin up,

This women,

Regal in her square,

Knowledgeable in her variances,

So assured,

That she is prepared to pour

Every drop of her love to give a pulse,

To stimulate your heart,

To increase your flow,

She delivers a portion at a time,

As your walk sets a course for unity,

She is fascinating,

Everyday elevating,

Bringing forth sweet delight,

For this experience,

When u enter her garden,

Do So Completely!

that's an ugly bruise

My, my, what happened to you?

Dragging low, she sick in the head, one said!

Oh my, that's an ugly bruise,

But who knew,

With as demure,

As back stretched, full length,

A comely smile to welcome anyone,

That behind closed doors,

The would be preacher,

Laid a tormented soul down for the evening whipping,

Oh my, what and ugly bruise!

For I blame religion,

I blame its rituals and traditions,

This development has retarded ones basic common sense,

So then they look on,

My what an ugly bruise,

A simple assessment,

Or better yet a psycho-social,

Would debunk the validity of this information,

It would demonstrate itself

Incapable of freeing this tortured soul,

But oh faithful,

Faithfully ignorant,

Though knees sore,

From hours of prayers to death ears,

Oh my, my, my, what an ugly bruise,

Upon what basis does one create this lifestyle?

Onlookers ranging new born on up,

The first teacher,

The Womb-man,

Relinquished her power

Given by the God-dess of the universe herself,

Who reached out with disparaged eyes?

My, my, my beloved daughter,

What an ugly bruise,

Unseen,

In the center,

What is perpetuated?

A never ending cycle of bruised knees, swollen eyes from hours of tears,

Hopeful intent,

Over the course of many years,

A disabled flight mechanism,

A false impression, and

Lowered standards of what an adequate mate is,

A continuity of continued falsification and jaded realities because cognitive dissonance persists,

So it is a wonder that one still says,

My, my, my what an ugly bruise you got there!

you have a right to your anger

These attempts to cause you to second guess yourself,

They should be futile,

Your reaction,

When you choose to have it,

Is classic text book,

They are the stages of grief,

You have a right to anger and frustration,

You are not making this up,

You have not falsified this information,

The emotions you feel are real,

No one will validate the contempt you are experiencing,

There is in fact a slighted distribution of goods, services, and opportunity,

Yes,

There is a hunt for your fathers, sons, and husbands,

This demon has manipulated seemingly intelligent people and made them enemies to one another,

For no reason other than the color of their skin,

For their religion,

For their finances or lack thereof,

You are entitled to your frustration,

They tricked you,

They robbed you of the ability to make educated decisions,

They intended that there should never be another Bacon's Rebellion,

Therefore lines of division were specifically renegotiated for this purpose alone,

They will ensure unity never reaches the hearts and minds of the masses,

For you all have been bamboozled,

Led astray,

At first,

You will reach a place of tremendous grief,

You will arrive at the road of immense guilt,

And this too is text book,

But take my hand,

Together will usher it in,

Truth,

Equality,

Progress,

And save all of humanity from eating itself from the inside out!!

You have a right to your anger,

Let no one ne'er again take your voice away,

Not even under threat of death,

For it is not the race card,

It is not a faint attempt to receive some preferential treatment,

Disallow this submission,

To stamp out your blackness,

Never again relinquish your stand for fear of reprisal,

Teach it with great vigor to your children,

Past it on by day,

For you are entitled to

Your anger,

For How does a man be a man in Africa?

Then upon that day that he reaches, against his will the new world,

Dust he cease to be a man?

How?

How is exactly,

To coddle you from the torturest reality that you yourself have sunk into a new low,

So low that one forces,

A man to be as a mule,

For and how does seemingly intelligent people not persist to the bottom of this great sin against humanity,

For what comfort does come from denying a man or woman or child a life,

At what cost does this impede your belly from filling?

At all this and bales more is your RIGHT TO your ANGER.

~~~~~~~~~~~~~~~~~~~~~~~~~~~~~~~~~~~~~~

Go With A Piece of Me!

My dearest heart,

My loving instrument,

Where goeth thou?

Into forever no more,

Alongside my mentor,

Brother minister Malcolm,

Give my love to him, for he too, gone to soon,

For you and ur journeying,

A tough terrain hath thou plowed,

I share some of the same,

We traveled some of the same miles,

Go with a piece of me,

For your gifts,

Unveiled a magnificence,

The blazing energy of woman,

You gave of your essence for all to see,

For all to examine,

It was your love that encouraged me,

A many day,

In this revelation, I think that I now know why caged birds have sung,

For I pay homage to you for allowing me your influence that I too may rise,

Into my place as a Phenomenal Woman!!

Dedicated to Maya Angelou- Go With A Piece Of Me, for You left so much of yourself behind

the third person

She maintains a little light,

Though she passed through her life like a flash,

From life's toils and turmoil,

Her childhood has been well preserved,

On intro, you do see a fully grown adult woman,

Somewhat weathered but yet still shining,

Hear this journey and it is a story that is larger than life,

This one person has survived all odds,

She fought and continues to stir,

Her eyes lend the most innocent and inquisitive,

The sweetest hint of that warm cuddly safe place that we all knew when we were young,

She holds it,

She accesses it,

She covers others with it,

Like a blanket, it caresses their skin and soothes their hearts,

Melts away their pain,

Her encapsulated little child, her other self, she is as new untouched, unweathered,

Happy she is,

To return,

Full and Complete.

... The more things stay the same

Hung from trees,
Those charred remains,
Lynched by police dead in broad day light, police brutality we claim,
No one stood in the balance for Emmett Till,
As such,
No one stood for Trayvon Martin,
Sean Bell, Anthony Baez, Eleanor Bumpers, Michael Brown, Eric Garner to name a few,
Fannie Lou hammer beat within inches of her life,
Eleanor Bumpers, A Grandmother,
Sat on her porch,
A sophisticated lynch mob went and shot that little old lady dead, got a promotion, 2 stripes,
but at the least for vindication we would have had him fired instead!

The more things change, The more things stay the same,
So how is that for progress?
Not particularly Jim Crow,
But redlined communities both, here, to and fro...
Hard working back breaking slave labor,
For your keep and meals,
To win the masters favor,
Brown nose,
Publicly berate your own people,

Sellout, Uncle Tom, Brown Noses,

Pats on the back in hopes of a promotion,

To deliver award acceptance speeches to rooms filled with other sheeple,

And as they say, the more things change,

The more they stay the same.

the power of the Pussy

After ur innocence is gone,
Some creep took it,
Be it selfishness,
Be it perverted,
Even be it for fun,
Its gone,

Upon every waking day,
A piece is churning,
Bit by bit,
It churns,
Then it sinks,
Even lower,
Still sinking,

And you surrendered the power of your pussy,

To derive control,
To say thank you,
To arouse jealousy,
For attention,
To feel pretty,
To experience love,
To be liked,

To belong,

It's the power of your Pussy,

Statistical data lied,
Those devil folks,
With their voodoo medicine,
They say u will be promiscuous,

You will be casting your precious pearl among swine,
Dogs it's all the same,

For the power of your pussy,

A higher probability of poverty,
And likely to be ignorant,
Detached emotionally.
Drug addicted,
Many babies,
Mood swings,
Single parent homes,

They wrote you to the grave,
Or cursed you forever to an invisible
Marginalized position,

For the power of your pussy,

All things under submission of the mind,
Perverse men, women, uncles, cousins, neighbors, father's, preachers,
priest, rabbis, gym teachers,

TORMENTED by their own guilt,
For you precious heart, you are free,
To wield the power of your pussy as u see fit...
They can not hold you prisoner,

Build your own stride,
Swag to your own drummers beat,

Girl, Lady, Woman, Sister, Daughter...

The power of your pussy,
TAKE IT BACK!!!!

so u like Black any other time

Black salmon
Black coffee
Black to look elegant
Black to ride in luxury
Black to get rid of the grey
Black for the exotic
Black incrusted diamonds
Black that leads a tuxedo
Black even to hide your gut
Black beautiful starry Night skies,
Black exclusive cigars
And
Black caviar
For u love BLACK any other time
Today, IT'S
Black Paula!

a Queen Deferred

A Queen Deferred,

Traveled the vast landscapes,

Encountering both peaks and valleys,

A queen in training returns,

Back from the wilderness,

True in her essence,

Proceeding to the light

To engage her reign,

wise and capable,

As a leader,

Powerfully,

Responsibly and Urgently,

As A deferred queen,

NO MORE!

Acknowledgments

A Queen Deferred- A Poetic Journey, Volume 1, has traveled the journey of title and concept for many years. Along the journey to fruition, i would like to thank a few people that have consistently supported me both through this work and through my personal growth. Candice, IS 72, Precious Bldg. 15, Rockia Robertson, Deborah Carraba, Vincent Grey, RIP, Renee Vashti, Denise, Eartha, Dawn Robinson, Kim, Errol, Charlie Rosenthal, thank you immensely to my Jewish Board and Family Services journey and family, by which were a pivotal part of personal development and absolute freedom to, "be", without judgment. Aunt Margaret Wilkerson and Cousin Russia, Atlanta, Ms. Grace, Harold Grace, Kendra and Shanshowa Dave, Tennessee love. Mr. Johnny Walker, Ms. Kerr, Ms. Douglas, Ms. Mandel, Ms. Cassidy, Immeasurable contributions, Thank you. Ms. Wilder, Ms. Cookie, Mr. Frank, Ms. Garrett, Ms. Odessa, Ms. Quack, Ms. Laura, And all my Madison street between Throop and Sumner Extended Family. Tonya Shemelle, Comedy Romance, Kizzy Samuel, My girl from way back, Karen Etheridge, My libra sis, Sasha Maharaj, kindred spirit sis, Khadijah James, My light sis, Pierre Horece, my haitian connection, Big Brother Mike, Always looks out, Brother Obama II, Ari, Sudan, Amadou Ndaiye, Senegal, Carly, UK, Dominique UK, Latoya Lunan, Fati, Max

Cohen, Joline, Max Regice, Aunt Mildred, Ms. Pearl, Papa Henri, Sapphire Howard, Robert Fenton, Hiromitsu, Japan, Velma Stoner, Leron Jenkins, Renee Sealey, Venus Torres, Denise Odin, Amal Mgaresh, Willie Irby, you have been in my corner 4 Ever, Traci Summers, Karen German, Minnie Faye Williams, Sgt. Lisa Washington, Georgia Department of Corrections, Roger McClellan, Tonawanda street. There are a few organizations that i feel compelled to list herein, The Salvation Army, Catholic Charities, The Jewish Board and Family Children Services, College of New Rochelle, Metropolitan College of New York, Momentum Education, Brooklyn Restoration Plaza, Blue Nile Tax Prep, thank you.

Made in the USA
Middletown, DE
07 February 2015